ANIMALS ON THE EDGE

GIANT Pandas in a SHRINKING FOREST

A Cause and Effect Investigation

by Kathy Allen

Consultant:
Colby Loucks
Deputy Director
Conservation Science Program, World Wildlife Fund

CAPSTONE PRESS
a capstone imprint

Fact Finders are published by Capstone Press,
151 Good Counsel Drive, P.O. Box 669, Mankato, Minnesota 56002.
www.capstonepub.com

 Books published by Capstone Press are manufactured with paper
containing at least 10 percent post-consumer waste.

Library of Congress Cataloging-in-Publication Data
Allen, Kathy.
 Giant pandas in a shrinking forest : a cause and effect investigation / by Kathy Allen.
    p. cm. — (Fact finders. Animals on the edge)
 Summary: "Describes giant pandas and their disappearing habitat"—Provided by publisher.
 ISBN 978-1-4296-5401-2 (library binding)
 1. Giant panda—Effect of human beings on—Juvenile literature.
 2. Giant panda—Conservation—Juvenile literature. 3. Endangered species—Juvenile literature.
I. Title.
 QL737.C214A39 2011
 599.789'168—dc22   2010033002

Editorial Credits
Mari Bolte, editor; Ashlee Suker, designer; Marcie Spence, media researcher;
    Eric Manske, production specialist

Photo Credits
Courtesy of Colby Loucks, 7, 8; Courtesy of World Wildlife Fund, 10; Getty
Images Inc.: China Photos, 26, Hoang Dinh Nam/AFP, 12, Peter Parks/AFP, 17;
iStockphoto: oversnap, 9; Nature Picture Library: Xi Zhinong, 25; Newscom: 13,
16, 20, AFP Photo, 14, CNImaging, 21; Peter Arnold, Inc.: E. Baccega, 22;
Shutterstock: Allan Szeto, 18, fenghui, 11, George Yu, 27, kldy, cover (panda),
Khoroshunova Olga, 6, Lynn Whitt, 4, Marc van Vuren, 23, Regien Paassen, 24,
ssguy, cover (bamboo), Worldphoto, 15, zhu difeng, 28; Wang Dajun/Wanglang
Nature Reserve, 19.

Printed in the United States of America in Stevens Point, Wisconsin.
092010   005934WZS11

TABLE OF CONTENTS

CHAPTER 1

Disappearing Giant Pandas

High in the forests of China is a quiet animal—the giant panda. Few people will ever see this creature in the wild. The giant panda is a bear, but it is quite different from other members of the bear family. It prefers to eat grass instead of meat. It lives alone, and it does not hibernate. Just one look at the panda's black-and-white face tells you that this bear is unique.

About 2 million years ago, the first giant pandas roamed China. But giant panda populations have been shrinking. Today there are only about 1,600 giant pandas in the wild.

Giant pandas are becoming more rare.

Giant Panda Range

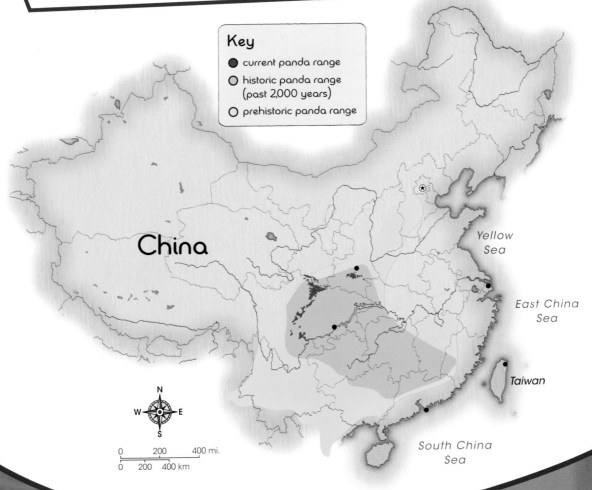

Key
- ● current panda range
- ○ historic panda range (past 2,000 years)
- ○ prehistoric panda range

China

Yellow Sea

East China Sea

Taiwan

South China Sea

N W E S

0   200   400 mi.
0   200   400 km

At 5 feet (1.5 meters) long, a wild giant panda can weigh as much as 250 pounds (113 kilograms). Adults have few enemies. When in danger, pandas swim and climb trees to safety. Pandas have learned to survive in China's high, misty mountains.

Unlike other bears, giant pandas eat mostly bamboo. Although pandas are able to eat meat, they prefer bamboo. Giant pandas have a large wrist bone that grips the bamboo **shoot** like a thumb. They use strong jaws and teeth to crunch the stalk. Pandas spend much of their day eating. And they eat a lot. One panda can eat 80 pounds (36.2 kg) of bamboo every day.

Scientists can identify individual pandas by the bite marks they leave on bamboo.

Pandas need to move to new patches to find edible bamboo. In the past, once an area of bamboo died off, pandas would move to a new area. Today this is not always possible.

shoot—a young bamboo plant

Bamboo forests grow in mountain ranges between 5,000 and 10,000 feet (1,500 and 3,000 m). Heavy rain, mist, and clouds provide unique growing conditions. Pandas are highly adapted to life in the bamboo forests. With so few pandas left in the wild, they may die out before adapting to a new habitat.

What Is Bamboo?

Bamboo is a woody grass. It thrives under forest cover. Although there is a lot of bamboo in the western Chinese mountains, it is not always ready to eat. Bamboo is a flowering grass. Large areas of bamboo die after flowering. Bamboo is the fastest growing plant in the world. But it can take years for bamboo to grow back after flowering.

The largest bamboo plant on record was 151 feet (46 m) tall. It only took a year for it to reach this size.

More than 1,000 kinds of plants thrive in bamboo forests.

So why are there so few giant pandas? What threats could such an animal face? Pandas need bamboo and space. Today there is less of both than ever before in China's western mountains.

As the bamboo forest disappears, pandas are becoming more exposed to humans.

People are now the greatest threat to giant pandas in the wild. Because of people, pandas are becoming **endangered**.

From 1974 to 1989, half of the pandas' **habitat** in China's Sichuan area was destroyed. People used the trees for firewood and timber. Farmers planted crops on the cleared land. The remaining forests were broken into smaller pieces by roads and people.

Surviving pandas live in about 20 patches of forest. The smaller patches prevent pandas from moving to find more food or a mate.

endangered—at risk of dying out

habitat—the place and natural conditions in which an animal lives

Pandas depend on the forest for food. Changes to the environment pose a huge threat to pandas' future.

But the forests need pandas too. Pandas are what is known as a **flagship species**. When a flagship species is protected, the plants and animals that share that species' habitat are also protected.

Pandas have also become symbols of conservation and endangered animals everywhere. They are some of the most popular animals in zoos around the world. Their story inspires animal lovers. People around the world are working to bring giant pandas back from the edge of **extinction**.

Pandas have been the symbol of the World Wildlife Fund since 1961.

flagship species—an animal chosen to represent an environmental cause

extinction—the act of dying out

Keeping a single panda in a zoo is expensive. A panda costs five times more to keep than the next most expensive animal, an elephant.

The Gift of a Panda

Pandas have long been used as political gifts. Between 1953 and 1982, 23 giant pandas were sent to nine different countries. Since the 1990s, pairs of pandas have been loaned to other countries at the price of $1 million a year. The pandas still belong to the Chinese government. Any cubs born overseas are sent back home to China to use in the country's breeding program.

America's public love of pandas began in 1936. That year, a panda named Su Lin arrived at the Brookfield Zoo in Chicago. Since then, there have been other pandas in the spotlight. In 1972 China gifted two pandas to the United States. The pandas, named Ling-Ling and Hsing-Hsing, made their home at the National Zoo in Washington, D.C. They came with bodyguards and crowds of fans. When the pandas died in 1992 and 1999, news media covered their passing. Today pandas still draw the biggest crowds at the zoo.

WHY ARE GIANT PANDAS ENDANGERED?

CHAPTER 2

A Human Threat

Humans are the main cause of the panda's habitat loss. More people are taking over the forests. Farmers climb higher in the mountains to plant crops such as corn. Roads cut through forests and mountains. All these people mean the loss of panda habitat. People have lived in China's mountains for thousands of years. But there are now more people sharing space with pandas than ever before.

More than 1.3 billion people live in China. It is the most populated country in the world.

Giant pandas need healthy forests to survive. They sometimes climb trees to escape predators or to rest. Female pandas use old trees as dens where they give birth and care for their young.

Logging destroys the giant panda's habitat. The trees that cover the panda's hills protect bamboo that grows under them. Often the bamboo is destroyed or does not survive once the trees are cut down. Logging in panda habitat has been outlawed since 1998. But some illegal logging still occurs. Sometimes farmers also burn the bamboo forests to increase the land for their livestock. And loggers, now out of a job, had to find other ways to make money. Some became **poachers**, buying and selling pandas and other rare animals in the illegal animal trade.

poacher—a person who hunts or fishes illegally

People have found more than 1,000 uses for bamboo, including wine, weapons, and instruments.

Giant pandas compete with humans for bamboo. People throughout southeast Asia eat bamboo. In the spring, bamboo shoots can be found in markets. The plants are used to make flooring, hats, tools, and medicine. Some people even live in houses made of bamboo. The leaves are used as livestock feed. The plant's main part is used as fencing material.

A pair of breeding pandas needs more than 11 square miles (28.5 square km) of land.

People build roads, fences, farms, and houses that pose more threats to pandas. The forests pandas live in are broken into pieces. The areas of bamboo can be as little as 1 mile (1.6 km) wide each. One giant panda typically needs between 2.5 to 4 square miles (6.5 to 10.4 square km) of land to survive. Pandas prefer living alone, but they need to travel to find mates. They sometimes travel to find food. Anything that keeps pandas from traveling between forest patches can be harmful. Manmade structures are just as deadly as habitat loss.

A panda fur can fetch between $60,000 and $100,000 on the illegal trade market.

Giant pandas have been seen as treasures around the world since the 1930s. The Chinese have valued pandas dating back as far as AD 685. That year pandas were used as a political gift from China to Japan.

But some people only see value in a panda's **pelt**. Poaching pandas for their skins was common in the 1980s and 1990s. Many laws have been passed to protect pandas. Until 1997, anyone found poaching giant pandas could face a death sentence. Today killing a giant panda in the wild can earn a person 10 years in jail. Even with strict punishments, panda pelts are still prized by illegal traders.

The bears sometimes get caught in traps. These traps are set for other animals like the Asian musk deer. The deer's oil is used in Chinese medicine.

pelt—an animal's skin with the hair or fur still on it

Coal provides 70 percent of China's energy needs.

Other manmade threats to pandas include coal mining and construction in panda territory. Even tourists can be a threat. Giant pandas are safest when they are unseen by people.

There is a fragile balance between pandas and humans. Both need places to live. Both call China their home. But one is facing extinction. If pandas become extinct, their loss could affect other forest animals. Takins, red pandas, musk deer, and leopards would be at risk. Much work must be done if giant pandas are to continue living in the wild.

WHAT CAN BE DONE TO HELP GIANT PANDAS?

CHAPTER 3

Saving the Giant Panda

The giant panda has been an endangered **species** since 1990. Groups around the world have been working even longer to protect pandas. The biggest threat to pandas is habitat loss. **Reserves** have been created as a safe place for pandas. In reserves, the land is protected from logging, mining, and the building of roads and farms. Today there are more than 50 panda reserves around the world. Reserve employees work with local communities to protect the panda's land. In addition, people are trying to connect panda reserves. By connecting reserves, pandas will have more room to live.

Scientists are hoping to increase the wild panda population to 5,000 by 2025.

Camera traps capture images of pandas living in their natural habitat.

Scientists also work in reserves to learn how pandas live in the wild. They try to learn more about pandas' needs. Workers in one reserve have set up camera traps. These traps automatically take pictures when pandas or other animals walk by. These pictures help count the number of wild pandas. The photos also teach us more about how pandas behave. Some wild pandas have been fitted with tracking collars. These collars allow scientists to monitor a panda's movements.

species—a group of animals with similar features

reserve—a place where animals can live and be protected from hunters and other threats

Panda reserves cannot succeed without the help of the people who live in or near them. Local people are learning safe farming methods that protect the land and the pandas. They plant trees to replace destroyed forests. They also patrol the reserves and guide tourists who come to see giant pandas. In some cases, farmers move away from the pandas' land.

Wild pandas are getting harder to find. Pandas are only able to mate for a couple days each year. If they have to travel long distances to find a mate, they may arrive too late. Pandas don't reach maturity until they are around 4 years old and sometimes not until age 8. They are past breeding age by 20.

Newborn panda

Newborn pandas only weigh 3 to 4 ounces (85 to 113.4 grams.)

Female pandas only give birth to one or two cubs. In the wild, a mother panda will only care for one cub at a time. Tiny panda cubs need a lot of attention from their mothers. Young pandas may stay with their mothers for as long as three years. This means that a wild panda may only raise three or four cubs in a lifetime.

More than 120 pandas have been born at the Wolong Panda Reserve.

It's cause for celebration when a panda cub is born. Today zoos and breeding centers work to keep a stable number of **captive** pandas. These pandas teach the public about their wild cousins.

The media has followed panda breeding in zoos for a long time. The first pandas that arrived in London and Chicago in the 1930s were big news. Zookeepers are learning more about how to help pandas reproduce. It is not an easy job. Pandas seem to have a hard time mating in captivity, and so rarely give birth in zoos.

Pandas have no problem raising cubs in the wild in ideal conditions. It is only in zoos where pandas have the most trouble breeding. Giant pandas, like all animals, behave differently when they are in captivity. But once cubs—especially twins—are born in zoos, they have a better chance at survival. Zookeepers can often help the mother keep both twins alive. They can make sure each cub gets enough food.

Today 90 percent of baby pandas born in captivity survive.

WHY SHOULD WE KEEP HELPING GIANT PANDAS?

captive—the condition of being kept in a cage

CHAPTER 4

The Giant Panda's Future

Between 1996 and 2006, the San Diego Zoo spent an estimated $30 million on its panda exhibit.

The work that has been done to help the giant panda has paid off. While there are only about 1,600 giant pandas in the wild, it is 40 percent more than in the 1980s. Logging and poaching are also much less of a threat than they were 10 or 20 years ago. Scientists and even zoo visitors know more about pandas than ever before. The efforts to save pandas educate people around the world. People can see what can be done to prevent extinction.

Animals who share the giant panda's habitat, such as the snub-nosed monkey, are also at risk.

Because pandas are cute and roly-poly, people are more sympathetic to their cause. But other species live in the bamboo forest. They benefit from the giant panda's star power. These animals include the red panda, snub-nosed monkey, and takin.

There is still work to be done if pandas are to survive. Without panda reserves and the cooperation of people, panda numbers will continue to shrink. Although panda cubs have been born in zoos, they need the most help in the wild.

Giving time and money to panda support groups is one way to help. Reading and learning more about pandas is also important. This knowledge will help people understand how to help pandas in the future. The hard work of teachers and scientists has been recognized. Today the giant panda is a symbol of how humans can work together to help animal conservation.

Learning more about why pandas are important is the first step to saving these gentle giants.

The panda is known as China's national treasure.

Life in the Bamboo Forests

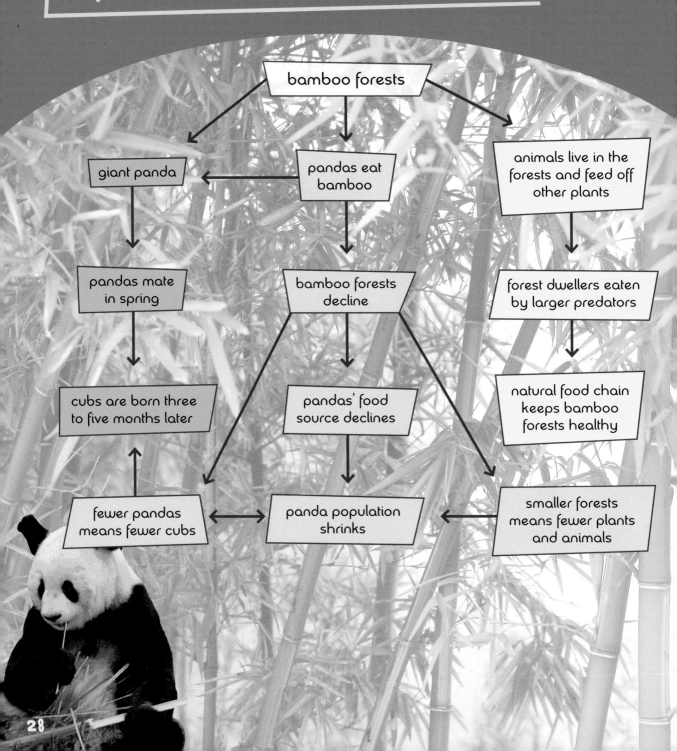

bamboo forests

giant panda

pandas eat bamboo

animals live in the forests and feed off other plants

pandas mate in spring

bamboo forests decline

forest dwellers eaten by larger predators

cubs are born three to five months later

pandas' food source declines

natural food chain keeps bamboo forests healthy

fewer pandas means fewer cubs

panda population shrinks

smaller forests means fewer plants and animals

RESOURCES TO HELP PANDAS

INTERNATIONAL ASSOCIATION FOR BEAR RESEARCH AND MANAGEMENT

The International Association for Bear Research and Management is a nonprofit organization that brings people interested in helping bears and their habitats together. With more than 550 members in over 50 countries, the IBA supports research and education on all bear species.

THE NATURE CONSERVANCY

The Nature Conservancy works across the United States and in more than 30 countries. With more than 1 million members, the organization works to protect both land and water habitats around the world.

WORLD WILDLIFE FUND

The world's leading conservation organization, the World Wildlife Fund encourages people to take action at every level—local and global Working in 100 countries, the WWF has more than 5 million members worldwide who work to educate people about conserving the world around them.

Glossary

captive (kap-TIV-ih-tee)—a person or creature being kept in a cage

endangered (in-DAYN-juhrd)—at risk of dying out

extinction (ik-STINGKT-shun)—the act of dying out; an extinct animal is one that has died out, with no more of its kind

flagship species (FLAG-ship SPEE-sheez)—an animal chosen to represent an environmental cause, such as an ecosystem in need of conservation

habitat (HAB-uh-tat)—the natural place and conditions in which a plant or animal lives

pelt (PELT)—an animal's skin with the hair or fur still on it

poacher (POHCH-ur)—a person who hunts or fishes illegally

reserve (ri-ZURV)—an area of land set aside by the government for a special purpose, such as protecting plants and animals

shoot (SHOOT)—a plant part that is just beginning to grow

species (SPEE-sheez)—a group of animals with similar features

Read More

Firestone, Mary. *Top 50 Reasons to Care about Giant Pandas: Animals in Peril*. Top 50 Reasons to Care about Endangered Animals. Berkeley Heights, N.J.: Enslow Publishers, 2010.

Keller, Susanna. *Meet the Panda*. At the Zoo. New York: PowerKids Press, 2010.

Torres, John. *Threat to the Giant Panda*. On the Verge of Extinction. Hockessin, Del.: Mitchell Lane Publishers, 2009.

Internet Sites

FactHound , soffers a safe, fun way to find Internet sites related to this book. All of the sites on FactHound have been researched by our staff.

Here's all you do:

Visit *www.facthound.com*

Type in this code: 9781429654012

Check out projects, games and lots more at
www.capstonekids.com

Super-cool stuff!

Index